Elise's Tea Room and Recipes

*To Sharon,
Let tea warm
your heart,
Elise*

Elise's Tea Room and Recipes

Where Tea Warms The Heart

Elise Benavidez

Copyright © 2016 Elise Benavidez
All rights reserved.

ISBN: 1539053938
ISBN 13: 9781539053934
Library of Congress Control Number: 2016916461
CreateSpace Independent Publishing Platform
North Charleston, South Carolina

Dedicated to my loving husband, who has always been by my side, guiding and encouraging me to find my true self, and to my supportive family, who helped me along the way.

Acknowledgments

A special thanks to my son Juan-Lucas, who helped me navigate my computer. Without him, there would be no book. Thanks to Tom Underhill for the beautiful pictures of the front of the tea room, to Tyler Gay for additional pictures, and to John A. Royce for the mouthwatering pictures of food.

Foreword

I FIRST MET Elise as she skated around the ice rink, smiling and showing such joy and glee—not skating for herself but to give all the feeling of how wonderful flowing on the ice could be. Fifty years later, I am still privileged to see Elise showing joy and glee in providing her guests the wonderful act of doing tea. Yes, as Elise's husband—a name I have been called many times—I can truthfully say that it has been a most interesting adventure. Tea.

Elise Benavidez

Her love of all the wonder that surrounds doing tea—a beauty we share—transformed her from a doctor's and professor's wife into an executive chef; an owner whose tea room is visited by huge tour buses; a community icon with a place of great cultural importance; and my boss. Her vision of having a place where everyone could afford fine dining in a rich and luxurious surrounding was infectious. Our life changed to orienting our goals to service. We traded clinics for culinary school, traveling to tea rooms far and wide to obtain the truest picture of what is the perfect tea, listening to all and reading books of tea experiences past and present. Elise is obsessive about tea, and her husband and children fed this obsession. Elise never faltered, always keeping her favorite idiom in mind: "You only coast downhill." When the director of Elise's culinary school attempted to steal her away from her tea-room idea to become the chef to the Ritz-Carlton, without hesitation she threw herself into the vision she always had—her tea room. It is no wonder that Congresswoman Juanita Millender-McDonald and Elise became friends and world-renowned Artist Yuroz thought of her as his muse. Her skills as a chef were honed. To inspire guests to return for two decades, it takes unfathomable skill to execute sandwiches that draw praise of haute cuisine and to keep scones and other tea food items fresh and exciting.

Her recipes are an accumulation of her life experiences—in her search for the most meaningful tea she might give. This book is her way of sharing the wonder of doing tea for those whom she did not have the privilege of serving. If it seems that I am slightly making a case for her sainthood and that I am biased, being her husband, well, you may be right. But I have gotten to see how, twenty-one years later in the tea business and fifty years of loving Elise, that young girl with glee and joy is still at Elise's Tea Room, giving wonder to the guests of her tea room.

Marcos, Elise's husband

Contents

Acknowledgments · vii
Foreword · ix
Elise's Tea Room and Recipes Where Tea
Warms the Heart by Elise Benavidez · · · · · · · · · · · · · xv

Chapter 1	A Little Girl and Her Grandmother · · · · · · · ·	1
Chapter 2	The Early Years ·	7
Chapter 3	The College Years · · · · · · · · · · · · · · · · · · ·	13
Chapter 4	A Love Story ·	15
Chapter 5	Family ·	18
Chapter 6	The Tea Room ·	21
Chapter 7	A History of Tea and Women · · · · · · · · · · · ·	28
Chapter 8	Serving a Proper Afternoon Tea · · · · · · · · · ·	37
Chapter 9	Tea Etiquette and Entertaining · · · · · · · · · ·	40
Chapter 10	Elise's Tea Room Recipes · · · · · · · · · · · · · · ·	52

Elise's Tea Room and Recipes
Where Tea Warms the Heart
by Elise Benavidez

TEA AND ITS history are embedded in my soul and every fiber of my being. I grew up drinking tea and enjoying all of its traditions. As an adult, I longed to return to that childhood experience. In search of finding this feeling again, I recreated my own world of tea: Elise's Tea Room. In this special space, I've tried to capture some of the many facets of tea traditions and history—old-world decor, fine dining in the traditional British style, and accompanying culinary delights—for the enjoyment of tea enthusiasts. This book tells my life story from childhood to adulthood and how I got inspired to open a tea room. Also included is a history of tea; its traditions, including tea etiquette; and, finally, my treasured recipes that have remained a secret until now.

CHAPTER 1

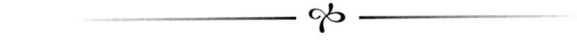

A Little Girl and Her Grandmother

THIS IS HOW the story begins. I was a little girl who loved her grandmother very much. My grandmother will never die because she will live on in my heart forever.

When I graduated from high school, she gave me a notebook that told her history, with information and dates found in her family Bible. This is the story from that notebook.

To tell the story, I must go back in time and start from the beginning with my great-grandmother. She was born Mary Olivia Lerrigo on March 2, 1868, in her home at 19 Queen Street in the small town of Hemel Hempstead, England. As a girl, she helped care for her four younger brothers while her older sister helped her mother with housework. Her family called her Lillie because she was very fair as a child. Later, she took Lillie as her legal name.

Mary Olivia Lerrigo (Lillie)

Her father was a contractor and had his own building contracting business. Times were hard for such a large family, and after he broke his leg, he decided to move his family to America to see if things would be better. All he could afford was steerage passage, but if it could bring better times, he knew it would be worth the hardship. In the summer of 1886, Lillie and her family arrived at Ellis Island in New York and made their way to Kansas. Her father found work in the carpentry business, and her brothers joined him when they got older.

On September 3, 1890, Lillie married the youngest son of a family that ran a hardware store in White City, Kansas. Three years earlier, her older sister, Annie, had married the second of the three Jones brothers.

Lillie found that married life was not all romance. One of the first presents her young husband gave her was a washboard. She cried.

Her brother Charles loved the sea and would take the family to California for vacation. Lillie and her husband enjoyed it so much that they decided to move to Los Angeles. In their new California home, they had four daughters, one being my favorite and beloved grandmother, Ethel Annie Jones, who was born on March 5, 1903, shortly after the family moved to Los Angeles.

Ethel's father bought a cow so the family could have enough milk, but soon they had too much milk, so he began selling the surplus. He added more cows, and later he moved the family to Downey, California, and opened a dairy farm. Ethel's most cherished childhood memories were of growing up on the farm.

In 1913, three days before Christmas, Ethel's father died. It was a very difficult time for her mother, and Christmas was, as my grandmother would always tell us, a very sad time for her. After his death, times were hard. Ethel's mother sewed, washed laundry, and canned fruit to make money to support her young girls. Religion always played a big part in Ethel's mother's life, and this helped the family through these hard times.

My grandmother went to school and became a teacher in Fillmore, California, where she roomed with some of her classmates. There she met Juan Catano Palacios, or John, who was born in Chihuahua, Mexico. In 1898, John and his family had fled Mexico to escape the revolutionary war led by Pancho Villa. They settled in Selma, California, under a program of the US government that offered immigrants citizenship in exchange for working on the railroads. John went to USC, which was a Methodist college at the time, to become a minister. He was appointed to a church in Santa Paula, California. John met Ethel in Fillmore while she was volunteering in his church as a Sunday-school teacher. She also played the piano during church services. They were married on June 30, 1926, one year after they met. They had two children: John (Jack) and Anita, my mother.

Ethel Jones, Sunday-school teacher
Fillmore, California

John and Ethel on their first date before their marriage, June 6, 1925

Elise Benavidez

John and Ethel, married June 30, 1926

CHAPTER 2

The Early Years

SUNDAY WAS ALWAYS a family day. After church, I would go to my grandmother's house for tea and treats. She had glass teacups with glass saucers that I would use to hold my treats on my lap while we visited.

My earliest memories are of spending the night at her house. It was a small, two-story house built by my grandpa, and it sat on a rolling hill. The kitchen was on the first floor and had a table that seated four and looked out onto the garden through sliding glass doors. The kitchen opened up to the living room, which had a wood burning fireplace that was always used in the winter. The living room also had an upright piano, a small couch, and two armchairs that faced the large window on the north side of the garden, where pots bloomed with orchids. There were two bedrooms and a bathroom upstairs. The first bedroom was the master bedroom, and the other was a spare. My grandma called the spare the blue room because it was painted the softest shade of blue. Grandpa had made built-in beds that could be turned into couches for use during the day. The blue room had a door that opened onto a balcony above the garage.

The best part of spending the night was after dinner when Grandma would draw a bubble bath for me. This was the biggest delight. She always had a box of individually wrapped Mr. Bubbles that came in a powder form and made bubbles as soon as it hit the water. After I had a long bubble bath, Grandma and Grandpa would tuck me into bed, with a kiss from each on the cheek. I remember that the house was a few blocks from the community hospital, and the ambulance siren in the middle of the night would be very frightening to me as a little girl.

In the morning, Grandma would fix a warm breakfast of eggs (egg substitute), toast, and fresh orange juice. This was always a treat, with my mother working and going to school at that time, I usually had cold cereal for breakfast. After breakfast, I would wash and dry the dishes and put them away. My grandmother would always say, "One person cooks, and the other one does the dishes."

In the afternoon, Grandma was always sewing. She made all her own clothes. She would lay out the material on a special cutting board made for cutting patterns, which had lines and measurements on the sides. She would put this on the dining table and pin her patterns to the material before cutting. She would let me help with the cutting, guiding my hand as I cut. With the leftover material, she made Barbie doll clothes for me. She also knitted slippers and afghans to give as gifts or to sell at the church bazaar. When I got older, she taught me how to sew and knit.

Late in the afternoon, it was nap time. After his heart attack in 1963, my grandfather would take a nap in the RV in the car park. I would go into the the RV for a few minutes to tuck him in, I loved my time with my grandfather, he always told me, "No matter what happens, always remember I love you." This stayed with me for the rest of my life and gave me great comfort. My grandpa was the only man who ever loved me unconditionally until I met my husband. But I'm getting ahead of myself—that comes later.

As I grew older, my grandparents were always there for me. I spent more and more weekends with them when my parents were getting divorced. A year after their divorce, my mother remarried. We moved to a new town where I went to a new school, but Grandma and Grandpa remained a source of stability in my life. My days at their house continued to follow the same schedule.

After my nap, I would play in the garden, which was like an enchanted garden. Being on a rolling hill, it had a top level and a bottom level. On the top level, Grandma had an herb garden with parsley, cilantro, garlic, and green onions for cooking. To reach the lower level, you had to wind your way through a path of steps cut from broken pieces of concrete made by Grandpa. At the bottom of the steps was a curving strip of grass. In the spring, the garden would pop with daffodils that my grandmother had planted in the fall. Grandpa got a duck named Daisy to eat the snails that plagued the garden. He would put the duck on his head, where she would sit happily, much to my delight. I was very saddened in 1972 that, after painting the little church he loved so dearly, Grandpa passed away from heart failure.

Elise Benavidez

Grandpa with Daisy the duck

Annie, my grandmother's china doll

Another favorite memory from my childhood was a special gift I received from my grandmother.

Charlie, my grandmother's uncle, and his wife would bring my grandmother trinkets from their trips abroad. After one trip, they brought her a china doll, which she named Annie (her middle name). She had stored it in a shoe box in her closet for years. When she felt I was of a proper age to care for the doll, she had her restrung, bought her a new wig, and made her a new dress. Then she gave her to me for Christmas. This doll is still one of my prized possessions—forever linked to a cherished memory of my grandmother.

Elise Benavidez

The times spent with my grandmother in my early years inspired me to open Elise's Tea Room. I wanted to recapture the intimacy and love I felt in sharing a cup of tea with someone special and to create a space for conversation, reflection, contemplation, and a chance to stop and relax.

CHAPTER 3

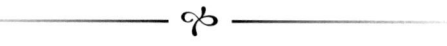

The College Years

I HAD GREAT sadness after my parents divorced, and I was very lonely. I began working with children in high school and decided I wanted to be a preschool teacher. I felt a strong sense of nurturing toward children and a bond of understanding. I attended Long Beach City College and majored in child development while working at Four Square Preschool in Garden Grove. I worked and studied hard, and I graduated in 1979 with an AA degree in child development. I soon became disenchanted with being a preschool teacher and decided not to open my own preschool because of the lack of value of the most precious human commodity, my time. I was in shock that I was often expected to extend my time without compensation—by the parents and definitely my superiors. I couldn't believe the unrealistic expectations of the parents in deferring the education of their children to me—without parental participation. I was expected—actually demanded—to pay for learning material from my minimum-wage salary. At this time, I was searching my soul for another path to take.

One day, I was at a jewelry store with my mother, and the jeweler noticed my interest in jewelry, suggested that I go to the Gemological Institute of America (GIA), and offered to give me a job when I graduated. So, with the encouragement of my mother, I took the jeweler's advice, moved to Santa Monica, and registered for the two-year program. The courses were very hard, and I would call home every Friday, worried and wondering how I would pass. But I made it through, and after graduating, I returned and began working at Mandarin Gems at the Westminster Mall in Westminster, California. I continued to work in the jewelry business, later appraising jewelry for insurance purposes. In June of 1980, my grandmother passed away from lymphoma. In 1982, I moved out of my mother's home and got my own apartment, which I shared with a roommate to split the costs. But even though I had a roommate, I was very lonely.

CHAPTER 4

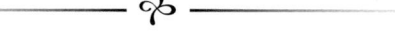

A Love Story

To tell this story, I have to backtrack a bit. In September of 1965, when I was eight, our family went to Lake Arrowhead for the three-day Labor Day weekend. My grandparents owned a cabin in Blue Jay that was a three-mile walk to Lake Arrowhead in the San Bernardino Mountains. A family from Latin American Methodist Church, where my grandfather was the minister and which we fondly referred to as the little church, had purchased land near Lake Arrowhead to build a cabin. We went to enjoy the Labor Day holiday and to help with the construction. But I don't know how much help we really were.

That Sunday, my dad took my three older brothers and me to the Blue Jay ice rink, and the boys from the other family met us there. My brothers chased me around the rink, teasing me and grabbing my knitted hat and skating away with it. My father had taught us all how to skate. I took to skating like a fish to the water.

When they announced the "Ladies' Choice" skate, I picked one of the boys from the other family. He was eleven years old, and he had been watching me the whole time. I held his hand all the way around the rink. He kept saying, "You are such a good skater." I was a much better skater than he was. That was our first meeting.

Years later, he told me that he fell in love with me on that day. He said it was the way I smiled at him. He told me that when he could drive at age fourteen, he began taking his motorcycle up to the mountains, hoping to find me, but he never could. Little did he know that we never went up to the mountains again. In addition, after my mother remarried, my stepfather adopted me, so I had a different last name, and with the move, he couldn't find me. To make matters worse, my grandmother had sold the cabin after Grandpa's death.

Sixteen years later, in 1981, we met again. He was teaching dance at an Arthur Murray studio in Orange County, and I was taking dance lessons at an Arthur Murray studio in Long Beach. Every year, there was a competition between dancers from all of the Arthur Murray studios in the region. It was called the Ball, and in 1981, it was held in Anaheim at the Inn at the Park.

When our eyes met, we recognized each other immediately. I said to my friend, "Wow, he grew up well," followed by, "I'm in trouble." He kept his eyes on me the entire time I was competing. After the award banquet, there was a dance at the end of the evening. He crossed the room toward me, never taking his eyes off me, and he said he was leaving for Oakland, California, in the morning. He had signed a contract to dance for the Oakland Ballet Company.

I didn't see him again until 1982 when we met at another dance competition; this time, he asked for my phone number. Three days later, on September 2—Labor Day weekend—he called me. It was a Saturday, and he called at 10:00 a.m. We talked for an hour, and he asked me out. He said, "So, would you like to get some breakfast?" We went to Huff's and talked over oatmeal. He told me that he fell in love with me at the ice rink in Blue Jay. The date lasted three days. He filled my loneliness. We were married in 1985.

Marcos and Elise, January 23, 1985

CHAPTER 5

Family

On Wednesday, January 23, 1985, we were supposed to meet with the pastor for marriage counseling at 3:00 p.m. that day. Marcos was attending a chiropractic college and had to miss his prudence class on prenuptial agreements. He was still working for the Arthur Murray studio to pay for his school expenses, and I was working at the jewelry store. In view of our busy schedule, we decided to forgo the counseling and have the wedding instead, leaving us only three days to prepare. I wore my mother-in-law's wedding dress, and we had a full church wedding. My mother cried and didn't understand why I was getting married on such short notice. Everyone in his family pulled together. My bridesmaid brought the flowers, his sister-in-law brought the cake, and his mother and I made the enchiladas for the reception. The reception was held at his parents' home and included dancing. The donation to the pastor was twenty-five dollars, and the food for the reception was fifty—the total wedding cost was only seventy-five dollars!

Soon after we were married, we were both fired from our jobs. He got fired for dating a student, even though I was a student at another dance studio—at least that was their excuse. I got fired because my mom had filed for a fictitious business-name license, in hopes of opening a jewelry store someday. It had been listed in a local newspaper per the filing process, and my boss thought I was in competition with him, even though I was unaware of my mother's post. So we started out our new life together with no money. Somehow we got along anyway. My husband did handyman jobs and washed cars, while continuing his studies, and I found a job as a gemologist.

We waited until April, during his school's spring break, to take our honeymoon. We drove his VW pop-top van to Yosemite. After six months of marriage, we were expecting our first son, who was born in April of 1986. With a new baby boy and a wife recovering from a C-section, he took his state board examination and passed with high scores. He started his own practice two years later. Soon it developed into multidisciplinary practice as we hired doctors, therapist, chiropractors and anesthesiologist. After working in the jewelry business for five years, I began working in his office, helping him with the billing and management of the business. When our son, Josue, was seven years old, he decided he didn't want to be an only child and asked for a brother. His brother, Juan-Lucas, was born in April of 1993.

Elise Benavidez

My Family

Josue and Chanthan, married December 12, 2009

CHAPTER 6

The Tea Room

THE MOST FREQUENT question I'm asked by my customers is: "What made you decide to open a tea room?"

My husband and I loved to have an afternoon tea, as we still do, but the only tea room at the time was located thirty miles east or thirty miles north of us. We enjoyed the traditions, luxury, and leisure that a tea room provides. Some of the tea rooms just "played tea." I longed for the style of a fine afternoon tea from the Victorian era with its particular feel and characteristics. So, out of necessity for a fine-dining tea room, and feeling that Long Beach needed a tea room, I opened one. The following is the story of how Elise's Tea Room came to be.

In May of 1996, my husband asked me if I ever wanted to own my own business. I responded that the only business I would like to have was a tea room. After a preliminary search of the different areas in Long Beach, I decided to locate the tea room in the historical neighborhood of Bixby Knolls. In June of that year, we opened Elise's Tea Room. Throwing caution to the wind—I had no restaurant experience—and with the support of my family, the tea room was born. There was no thought of failure, and so off I went.

Elise Benavidez

When I was first married, I didn't even know how to make coffee, and now I owned a tea room! We couldn't get a bank loan or funding, so we footed the bill with credit cards. We signed a ten-year lease with the building owner. At first, the menu was very small, just muffins and tea; we didn't know if the business would even succeed. Later, we added scones, sandwiches, and dessert. We also sold teapots, teacups, and tea accouterments.

After we had been in business for seven years, the owner of the building died, and the new owner didn't want a tea room there. The new owner raised the rent, even though we had three years left on our lease. There were only two choices: either close the tea room for good or move and create a new tea room. Three doors away, a flower shop in a very attractive building with bay windows was going out of business. I went over and talked to the owner who said he would be happy to have me as a new tenant. It turns out the building was the Ordinal Bixby Knolls Library, a landmark building—the perfect spot for a tea room.

I kept the old tea room open while the new tea room was being remodeled so as not to lose business. It took three months to complete. The floor plan had to be submitted to the city, along with a kitchen plan with the required five sinks, and all health department regulations needed to be met. My husband, brother in-law, and sons worked long hours building and laying tile. My older son had started working with me when he was fifteen years old, learning how to bake scones and, later, when he was eighteen, waiting tables. His younger brother worked in the tea room as well when he was old enough. My husband would come from his office during his lunch break and wash dishes.

The new tea room reopened in January, and with all the lessons learned from our first tea room, it was a great improvement. My older son met his wife at the new tea room; she was working for me at the time. He would come to visit me at the tea room for lunch, but he really was coming to see her. They were married on December 12, 2009.

One of my goals for the new place was to make the food even better—the scones less dry, the soups thicker, and the quiches fluffier—so I went back to school, this time taking culinary classes. I worked during the day at the tea room and attended classes at night. Eventually, I graduated with a hotel/restaurant management degree with baking and chocolate certification. My husband retired from his practice and went back to school with me. He received pastry and baking certification and became our pastry chef. This education greatly improved the quality of the food. From 2001 to the present, the tea room has received the Five-Stars Award from the Southern California Restaurant Writers, and in March of 2010, my husband received the Pastry Chef of the Year award.

In 2007, the jewelry store next door went out of business, and we took over the lease. Glad to have the extra space, we cut a hole in the wall between the two areas and went from one thousand square feet to two thousand square feet. With the help of my husband, sons, mother, and an interior decorator, we soon had a new room painted a light Wedgwood blue and decorated in the French style. Since the expansion, we've enjoyed hosting bridal showers, baby showers, intimate weddings, birthday parties, Red Hat groups, and the Bixby Knolls Literary Society in a room that is relaxing and elegant, with an old-world charm.

At the age of fifteen, our younger son started taking a piano class and discovered that he has a passion for and a love of music, especially music composition and theory. In 2010, he was honored to receive an 1896 Hamburg Steinway & Sons concert piano, in memory of his Grandfather. It features a rosewood case that was sent to Paris to be covered with 22K gold gilt and decorated with scenes from Wagnerian operas by the artist P. Juette. In more recent years, it resided in the presidential palace of Mexico City as an anniversary gift from President Mateo Lopez to his wife. The piano now resides in our French Blue Room (reminiscent of my Grandma's blue room.)

This new room has been the scene of many gatherings of intellectual, political guests, including councilmen, county officials, artists, musicians, and poets. My most treasured award is from the US House of Representative certificate of recognition, which states: "On the occasion of your twentieth anniversary, congratulations for your dedication to bringing a fine-dining and tea-time experience to Long Beach and for your outstanding commitment to our community."

The tea room is constantly changing and improving itself. Last year, we installed a dance floor, where Chef Marcos, a dance instructor for more than thirty-five years, teaches ballroom dance classes on Thursday night.

Elise's Tea Room and Recipes

An 1896 twenty-two-carat gold, gilded Steinway & Sons concert piano

Elise Benavidez

Above are Elise's Tea Room staff members that have been with the tea room for longer than five years. Thank you for your loyal service. From left to right: Sam, Chef Marcos, Elise, Juan-Lucas, Tyler, and Ricardo.

Picture by Tom Underhill

Chef Marcos makes beautiful cakes for weddings, bridal showers, and birthdays.

CHAPTER 7

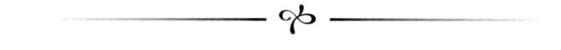

A History of Tea and Women

THERE ARE MANY myths and legends in the history of tea, such as those regarding who was the first to discover the benefits and pleasures of drinking tea. The most well-known legend, and my favorite tale, is that of the emperor Shen Nung in 2737 BC. While traveling and surveying the borders of his territory, the Chinese emperor stopped to rest and put a pot of water on to boil. In ancient times, gas stations, restaurants, and hotels couldn't be found on every corner. When you left your home to travel, you had to camp out. The emperor was extremely innovative for his time; he was determined to enlighten his people regarding the virtues of a disciplined and wholesome lifestyle. He passed strict laws to expedite the enlightenment. For example, citizens of China were ordered to boil all water before drinking, for reasons of purity.

As he rested, Shen Nung used a nearby bush to make a fire and noticed that leaves had fallen into the pot and stained the water. Being an avid herbalist, he tasted the infusion. And he pronounced it good. The shrub that shed its leaves into Shen Nung's water was the wild ancestor of *Camellia sinensis*, the source of all modern tea (with the exception of herbal infusions). Upon his return, Shen Nung immediately commenced the large-scale cultivation of tea in China. The people of China, trusting their benevolent emperor, began drinking tea in earnest. After water, tea is the most-consumed beverage on Earth.

Portrait of the Red Emperor, Shen Nung (2838–2698 BC)

We drink virtually the same tea today that Emperor Shen Nung drank the day he discovered it.

The tea plant is a perennial evergreen shrub of the genus *Camellia sinensis*. It can grow to up to forty feet, but it is trimmed to waist height to make it easier to pick the leaves.

In the Jingmai Mountain area of China, there is an ancient tea plantation. The tea trees spread out over 11,000 acres of mountains. The ancient tea forest of this mountain is located approximately 5,000 feet above sea level and is blanketed in mist. The rich soil and climate are especially suitable for the growth of the tea trees. Tea cultivation in this area began over 1,300 years ago. Experts have verified that these ancient tea trees are between 800 and 1,200 years old. It is the largest ancient tea plantation ever found in China that is still producing tea today. The region has been recognized as a natural tea museum.

Three major classes of nonherbal tea come from the *C. sinensis* plant: 75 percent is black, 23 percent is green, and 2 percent is oolong. Tea leaves are green at harvest, and to achieve the three different types that the industry demands, the manufacturers control the length of time the tea leaves are exposed to air. This process is called fermentation. When fermentation is completely stopped, the tea leaves stay green or yellowish brown. When the fermentation time is long, the leaves darken and become black. Between these two extremes is oolong tea.

Many health benefits have been associated with drinking tea. Because the plant grows in the sun, the plant protects itself against photosynthetic stressors by forming chemicals known as polyphenol antioxidants. In April of 2004, the US Department of Agriculture (USDA) conducted a study on tea and bone mineral density in older women. The results of the study showed that women who drank tea had higher bone mineral density measurements; thus, tea may protect against osteoporosis. Tea may also help in lowering cholesterol levels. The USDA continues to conduct studies on health benefits of drinking tea.

Tea was first introduced to Portuguese priests and merchants in China during the sixteen century. The first tea to arrive in Europe was in 1610 by the Dutch trade ships. The heavy taxation had the effect of creating a whole new industry, tea smuggling. The ships from Holland and Scandinavia brought tea to Britain. The ships stood offshore while the smugglers unloaded the tea into small vessels, often manned by local fishermen.

In the early 1800s, ships carrying tea from China to Britain could take up to a year in transit. When the East India Company was given a monopoly on tea trade in 1832, the Dutch realized they needed to cut the travel time of their journey, so they built clipper ships for speed. A common misconception is that Marco Polo brought tea back from China, but tea was acquired via the Silk Road much later, as mentioned in a book by Rustichello da Pisa, *The Travels of Marco Polo*, that he wrote about the stories told to him by Marco Polo.

In 1661, Catherine Braganza of Portugal married Charles II. As part of her dowry, she brought tea and accessories to introduce the drinking of tea in England, a custom that was already common among the Portuguese nobility of the time. Although she was not a particularly popular choice for queen (because she was Roman Catholic and because of the language barrier), her quiet decorum, loyalty, and genuine affection for Charles changed the public's perception of her.

Oddly enough, the London coffee houses were responsible for popularizing tea in England. By 1700, over five hundred coffeehouses sold tea, cutting the ale and gin sales of tavern owners. It was also bad news for the government who relied on the revenues from the liquor sales tax. Charles II put several acts into place that forbid tea sales in private homes. This tax was unpopular and impossible to enforce. A 1676 act taxed tea and required coffeehouses to apply for a license to serve it.

Maria Tewkes of York, 1700–1725, was the first female tea merchants. She was single and said to be very single-minded. Not much is written about her, and most histories of tea leave her out altogether and skip straight to Mary Little Twining.

The founder of Twining Tea Company was Thomas Twining. He opened the first-known tea room in London, in 1706, which still operates today. Mary Little Twining married Daniel Twining in March 12, 1762. She inherited the business after her husband's death. It flourished for seventeen years.

Following the historical timeline, in December 16, 1773, the Boston Tea Party occurred. One of the stories from Wikipedia states that, in defiance of the Tea Act of May 10, 1773, American colonists, dressed as Native Americans, threw an entire shipment of tea from the East India Company into the Boston Harbor, leading to the American Revolution. They dumped 342 chests of tea into the water—an estimate of one million of today's dollars. After reading a letter from John Adams to Abigail Adams, dated July 6, 1774, I discovered that women in Boston, Massachusetts made a protest of the Tea Tax. In the letter John Adams Stated and I quote, "Tea must be universally renounced." Also in his letter is the following: "When I first came to this house, it was late in the afternoon, and I had ridden thirty-five miles at least. 'Madam,' said I to Mrs. Huston, "is it lawful for a weary traveler to refresh himself with a dish of tea, provided it has been smuggled or paid no duties?,' 'No, sir,' said she, 'we have renounced all tea in this place. I can't make tea, but he can make you coffee.'"

Women in 1773 were given an allowance to buy the household supplies and were expected to make a home with whatever was provided by their husbands. With the tax on tea, the women protested by refusing to buy tea. Perhaps, as stated in the previously reference letter from John Adams to his wife, the men were pressured into protesting by tossing the tea overboard, so they would not disappoint their wives.

As a female owner of a tea room, I find it interesting that women were the first to introduce the refined customs of drinking tea, starting with Catherine Braganza and then Ann Maria Russell, the Duchess of Bedford.

The Duchess of Bedford was a lifelong friend of Queen Victoria. She served as Lady of the Bedchamber between 1837 and 1841 and was considered to be the originator of the British " afternoon tea." In the nineteenth century, Ann Maria Russell, who was too hungry to wait for the 9:00 p.m. dinner hour, began requesting a bit of bread and butter, biscuits, and cakes to enjoy with her afternoon tea. When the queen found out, she instantly loved the idea. The duchess found taking an afternoon tea to be such a perfect refreshment that she soon began inviting her friends to join her. The tradition of afternoon tea started.

Anna Maria Russell, 1839, Duchess of Bedford

Traditionally, afternoon tea is loose tea brewed in a teapot and served in teacups with milk and sugar. The tea is served with tea sandwiches with such fillings as cucumbers, eggs, watercress, and cream cheese with chives and ham. Scones are also served, with accompanying Devonshire cream, jams, and lemon curd. Dessert consists of fruit tarts, lemon tarts, cakes, and petite fours, often served on a three-tiered stand.

High tea is generally served on farms for the workers who come in from the fields between 5:00 p.m. and 6:00 p.m. It largely consists of tea served with cold meats, eggs, or fish.

The demand for tea increased, and in 1849–1842, the First Opium War began.

With the demand for Chinese goods (silk, porcelain, and tea), there was an a imbalance in trade. The British East India Company began to auction opium, grown on its plantations in India, to China. The increasing number of opium addicts alarmed Chinese officials. In 1839, the Daoguang emperor made opium illegal. The British government, not officially denying China's right to control imports of the drug, objected to this unexpected seizure and used its naval forces and gunnery to inflict a quick and decisive defeat.

Customs have changed over the years. Today, most men and women work until 5:00 p.m., making it more difficult to enjoy an afternoon tea. Tea is still widely popular as a soothing beverage, and the unique way of drinking it has developed in different places, each creating its own customs.

Tea has played an important role in history over the years. In the United States, it is associated with the family gathering around the kitchen table for a cup of tea or at night before bed. Tea is not only for grandmothers, as it is sometimes equated with, but it's popular with all ages. To this day, coffee remains more popular than tea in the United States; however, the US still consumes 7.8 gallons of tea per capita annually. Some people still long for the Victorian style of tea service. Serving an afternoon tea brings us back to Victorian customs; civility; and a feeling of sophistication, leisure, and luxury.

Elise, serving a traditional afternoon tea

CHAPTER 8

Serving a Proper Afternoon Tea

WHO KNEW HOW complex serving a proper afternoon tea would be? Inviting a few friends over for tea, or even hosting a tea party at your home, can involve several different protocol and customs. Here are five steps to serving an afternoon tea.

Step 1: Supplies

Make sure you have all the supplies you need. You will need a tea pot or two, depending on the amount of different flavors of tea you are serving; cups and saucers; creamer; and sugar. You will also need a nice linen tablecloth; napkins; and a serving platter or a tiered tray.

Step 2: Making a menu

Tea sandwiches, scones, and cakes are favorite afternoon tea items, passed down in history by the Duchess of Bedford. You can purchase supplies to make savory delights or have the food catered. Supplies can be purchased the day before.

Step 3: Making tea

Heat the water on the stove in a kettle or pot. Bring the water to a brisk boil. While waiting for the water to boil, rinse the teapot with warm tap water to prevent the pot from cracking from the shock of the hot water and also so it keeps the water hot—a cold teapot would drop the temperature of the water.

Step 4: Adding the tea leaves

Use about one tablespoon of tea per person, depending on how strong you want your tea. At the tea room, we use one tablespoon for a small pot and two tablespoons for a large pot. Pour hot water into the pot. If using loose tea, you will need a strainer over each cup to filter the tea leaves. You could also use a tea sock or a tea ball.

Steep the tea for three to five minutes. Green tea takes longer to brew. If the tea gets too strong, add hot water to the pot. Provide your guests with milk, lemon, sugar (sugar cubes are preferred), honey, and sweeteners. Milk was first added in Victorian times to prevent the fragile porcelain cups from cracking. With today's cups, milk can safely be added afterward.

Step 4: Tea sandwiches, scones, and cakes

The Earl of Sandwich was credited with inventing the sandwich. It was named after John Montagu (1718–1792), the fourth Earl of Sandwich, who ordered his valet to bring him meat tucked between two pieces of bread. Then others began to order "the same as Sandwich." In Britain, tea sandwiches are served first; a few examples include chicken curry, egg, cucumber, chives, and a favorite of Queen Elizabeth II, butter with jam. The sandwiches are served with the crusts cut off and are small enough to eat with your fingers.

Next come the scones, followed by sweet items, such as bite-sized cakes, fruit tarts, and petite fours.

Step 5: Host or hostess

When serving family or close friends, the host or hostess plays "mother" and is expected to serve the first cups of tea. After the first cup of tea, the guests can share the job of pouring.

CHAPTER 9

―――― ❦ ――――

Tea Etiquette and Entertaining

Etiquette

WHAT IS ETIQUETTE?
THE TERM *ETIQUETTE* means "ticket or card." It refers to the ancient custom of a monarch setting forth the rules and regulations for the members of the court. Rules and regulations are still a major part of our daily lives.

The essence of etiquette is civility. *Civility* means "politeness." Civility involves thinking about others and how they feel and act as well as being considerate and displaying sensitivity.

The more you practice being good to people, the more it becomes second nature. There are many things you can do to make life more pleasant for you and others. Here are a few examples:

- Say hello to the people you encounter.
- Use *please* and *thank you*.
- Shake hands when you meet someone.
- Show respect for older people.
- Respect others' privacy.

- Speak when spoken to.
- Don't interrupt during a conversation.
- Be quiet in public places.
- Don't complain.
- Don't touch or play with other people's possessions unless given permission.
- Get along with others.
- Be a good friend.

Cary Grant was born poor; he did not have the finer things in life. He once said, "I acted like a gentleman so long I finally became one." If you act like a gentleman or lady long enough, you will also become one.

The following guidelines cover the basics of etiquette: manners, introductions, polite conversation, and personal appearance.

MANNERS

The term *manners* refers to the way in which something is done or the way you behave. Having good manners gives you a sense of confidence. With manners, having warmth and sincerity is more important than knowing the strict protocol. Manners help us feel at ease and give us self-esteem. Manners are created by society and therefore can differ by culture, but one simple rule always applies: treat others with as much kindness and courtesy as you would like them to treat you.

Telephone manners and table manners are important aspects of manners; here are some guidelines:

Telephone manners

- Turn off your cell phone at the table.
- Don't text—give your full attention to your companion or guest.
- When calling a friend and someone else answers, be polite and say, "Hello, this is Sally. May I please speak to Mary?"

Table manners

- Wash your hands before coming to the table.
- Put your napkin in your lap.
- Sit up straight.
- Wait until everyone is served before eating.
- Ask politely for dishes or condiments to be passed; never reach across the table.
- Keep your elbows off the table.
- Never chew with your mouth open.
- Never talk with your mouth full of food.
- Use your spoon quietly when stirring your tea; never bang your spoon on the teacup.
- Ask to be excused from the table if you need to leave.

Introductions

Knowing when and how to make introductions is a part of good manners. Here are some guidelines:

- Introducing someone else: Add something about the person along with the name—for example, "Sue, I'd like you to meet Mr. Smith, my history teacher," or "Mr. Smith, I would like you to meet Sue; she is in my English class."

- Shaking hands: The purpose of the handshake is to convey warmth and feeling between two people. The way you shake hands is considered an indication of your personality. A weak handshake translates as a wishy-washy person, whereas a firm handshake says you are someone with character. But don't be too firm—you also don't want to crush the person's hand.
- Forgetting a name: This happens to everyone at some point. The best thing to do is to be honest and say, "I'm sorry—your name has gone straight out of my head."
- Greeting an acquaintance: Don't ask, "Do you remember me?" It's considered tactless because it puts the other person on the spot.
- Being called by the wrong name: Correct the error right away—for example, "I'm sorry to interrupt, but my name is Elise, not Elsie."

Polite conversation

Don't interrupt a person; it's rude. Being a good listener is the nicest thing you can do. Here some additional guidelines for polite conversation:

- Don't talk too much.
- Don't talk down to people or above their heads.
- Show respect.
- Pay a compliment or express a happy thought.
- Respond to a compliment—for example, "It's so nice of you to say so."
- Don't ask how much something cost; it's considered poor manners.
- Admit when you're wrong; you will gain respect, and it may save a friendship.

- Apologize when you are at fault; say that you are sorry, and add an explanation.
- Accept an apology, which may be hard, but for the sake of the friendship, accept it with grace.
- Stand up for a friend—never let a friend be criticized unfairly, and point out the friend's positive attributes.

Personal appearance: Hygiene

The way you dress tells a lot about you. Your appearance and the way you dress make the first impression. What's important is how well groomed you are, not whether you're wearing the newest fashion. Are you neat and clean, and do you smell pleasant? Grooming refers to the way you care for your body, and further guidelines should be followed when serving food:

- Wash your hands.
- Keep your hair clean and well combed; you shouldn't look like you just crawled out of bed. When working in the kitchen or serving food, hair should be tied back or up so that hair doesn't fall into the food.
- Use deodorant.
- Keep your fingernails clean; remove chipped polish.
- Wear closed-toed black shoes with a low heel. Tennis shoes are not appropriate.
- Wear a white shirt that is clean and ironed.
- Wear black pants that are clean and ironed—no blue jeans.
- If you have a cat or dog, remove all pet hair with a lint brush.
- Use good posture: stand up straight, shoulders back, chest out, eyes forward.
- Pick up your feet when you walk. Don't shuffle your feet.
- Don't chew gum.

Few people can ever hope to remember every single aspect of etiquette, but keep in mind that it won't be the end of the world if you use the wrong fork. Just remember to be sincere and treat others with warmth and kindness, and you're on your way to having good manners.

Entertaining: How to host a dinner party

When hosting a dinner party, there are many factors you must consider:

- What is your budget? How much are you prepared to spend?
- How many guests are you planning to invite?
- Where will you hold the dinner party? The number of guests will determine your location.
  - Is your home/apartment large enough to hold your guests comfortably?
  - Do you have enough tables and chairs to seat your guests?
  - Consider renting a hall, banquet room, or church facility if your place isn't big enough.

THE INVITATION

The invitation must include the following:

- date
- time
- place
- RSVP—an abbreviation for the French phrase *répondez s'il vous plaît* ("please respond")

Note that you should not use the Internet to send invitations for formal dinner parties. Use standard mail to send out the invitations three weeks before the party—or four weeks during the holiday season.

Menu

After you decide on the number of guests you plan to invite and the location, the next thing to decide is the menu. This also depends on your budget. Check store ads and restaurant supply stores, and make a list of prices before buying your supplies.

Five-course menus are rarely served today. People are concerned with weight gain and also don't want to spend endless hours at a dinner table. A four-course meal is now more common:

- first course—soup or consommé
- second course—salad
- third course—main dish
- fourth course—dessert

Beverages

Make a list of the beverages you wish to serve:

- tea
- coffee
- decaffeinated beverages

Assign a staff member or server to be in charge of the beverages.

Equipment

Make a list of the equipment you will need:

- number of tables
- number of chairs
- amount of flatware: forks, knives, spoons, soup spoons, salad forks

- number and types of dishes:
- soup bowls
- salad plates
- main-dish plates
- dessert plates
- number of water glasses
- number of coffee cups or teacups
- tablecloth and napkins:
  - number and color of tablecloths, most use white or ivory
  - number, color, and folding style of napkins—this number should be according to how many guest and a few extra

SETTING THE TABLE

The table can be set the day before if the space is available. This can save you time and make the day of the event less stressful.

- Place the tablecloth on the table first, making sure that it does not touch the chairs, tucking and securing it under the table if necessary—this prevents guests from accidentally pulling the tablecloth when they sit down.
- Fold the napkins and place each napkin centered just above the chair and one inch up from the edge of the table.

TABLE SETTING

- Set the water glass above the knife (see accompanying illustrations).
- Set the teacup or coffee cup above the spoon, with the handle at a ninety-degree angle.
- Set each table with sugar, sweetener and honey, salt and pepper, and creamer for coffee/tea.

- Include attractive centerpieces. Arrangements for the center of the table add a festive look. Make sure arrangements or centerpieces are low enough so that guest can see one another.
- Place a menu card on each table if desired.
- Decide whether you're going to have a seating chart, and if so, place name cards on the table above the napkin.

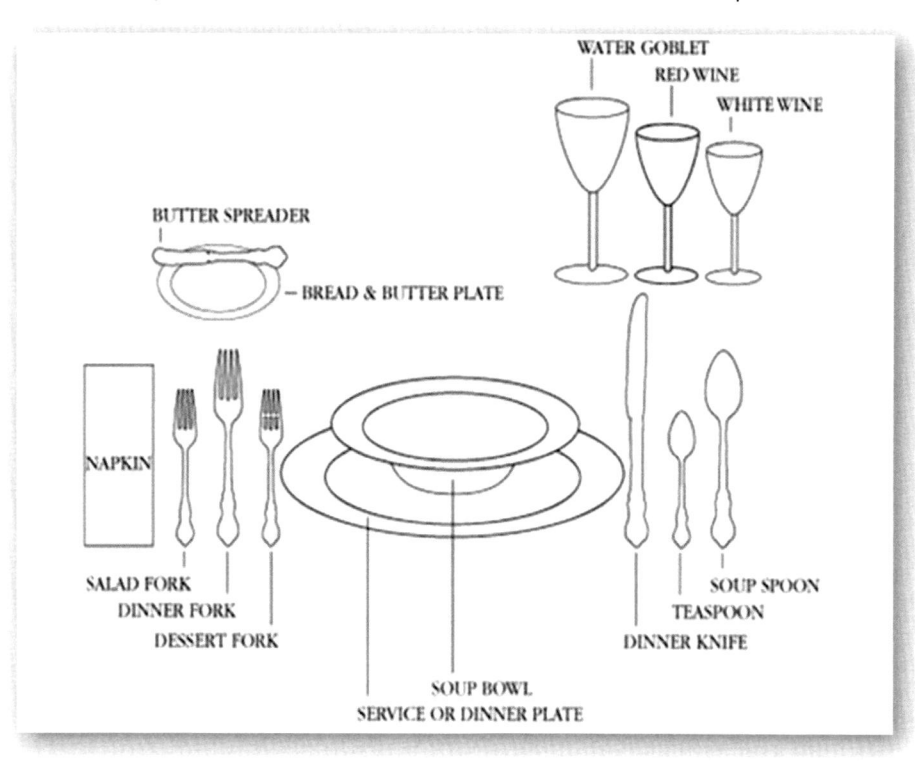

Elise's Tea Room and Recipes

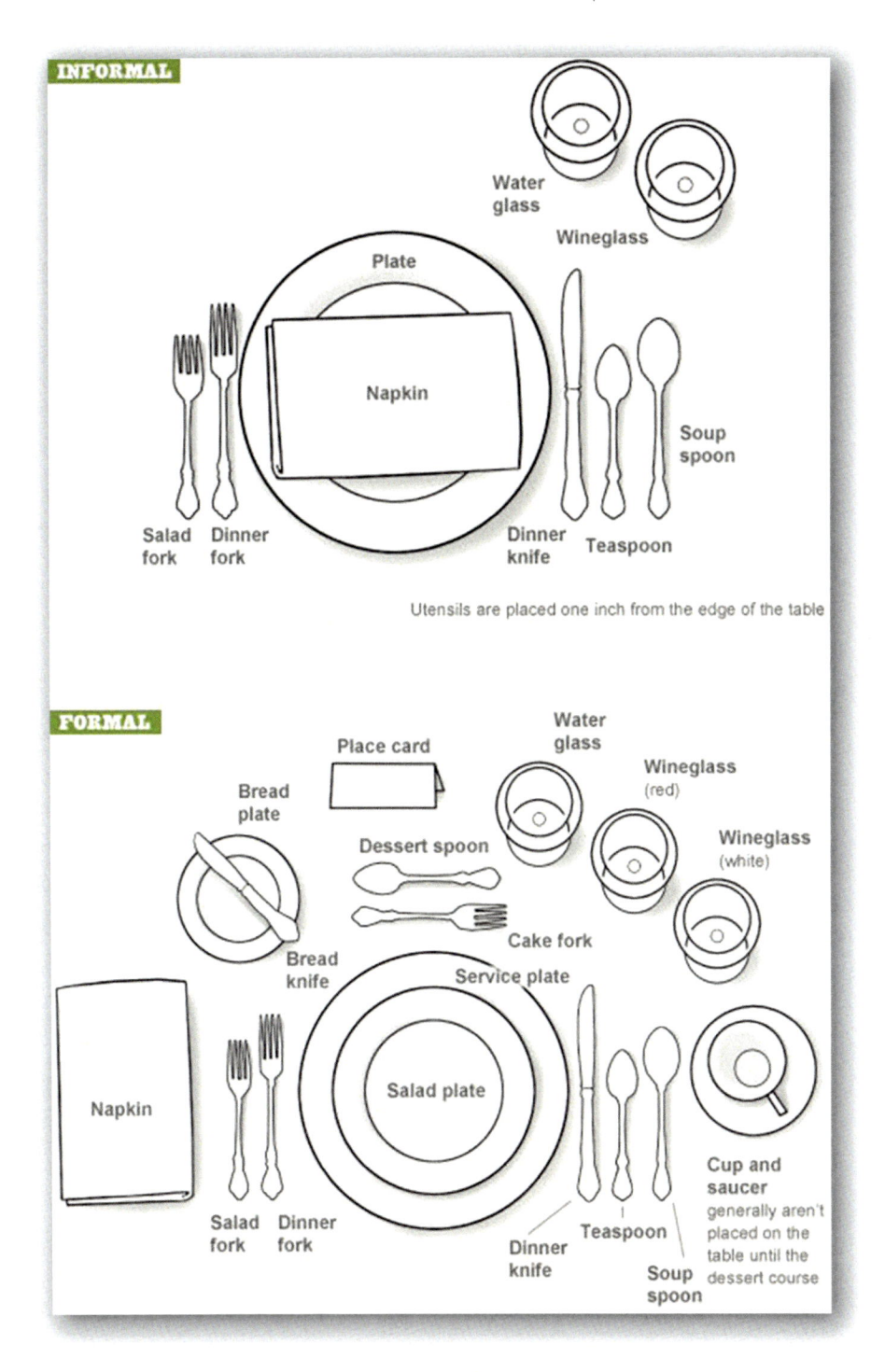

INFORMAL

- Water glass
- Wineglass
- Plate
- Napkin
- Salad fork
- Dinner fork
- Dinner knife
- Teaspoon
- Soup spoon

Utensils are placed one inch from the edge of the table

FORMAL

- Place card
- Water glass
- Wineglass (red)
- Wineglass (white)
- Bread plate
- Dessert spoon
- Cake fork
- Bread knife
- Service plate
- Salad plate
- Napkin
- Salad fork
- Dinner fork
- Dinner knife
- Teaspoon
- Soup spoon
- Cup and saucer generally aren't placed on the table until the dessert course

49

FINAL PREPARATIONS

Make a checklist of things to do a week before the party:

- Review the facility layout (if not at your home).
- Check and count all dishware.
- Count flatware.
- Count glasses and make sure they are washed.
- Check tablecloths for spots and iron if wrinkled.
- Count and check centerpieces.
- Write or print menu cards for each table.
- Check lighting—are you going to use candles?

SERVICE

- Serve beverages first.
- Serve beverages on the right-hand side, and pick them up on the right-hand side.
- When serving food, serve from the left, and pick up from the right.
- Smile when you leave the kitchen.
- Be prompt when serving so that the food stays hot, but be careful to avoid slips and spills.
- Check with the host for the time to start serving. A prayer or blessing may be customary.
- Stop what you're doing and serve. All servers should serve at the same time to speed up the delivery of the food.
- Pick up plates and check needs of guests.
- Continue serving courses—when everyone is served, begin preparing the next course.

Cleanup

If you are hosting an event at a rented facility, the following guidelines apply:

- Remove all dirty dishes from tables.
- Stack chairs.
- Fold up tables and store, if applicable.
- Vacuum after all guests have left.
- Take out all trash.
- Turn off ovens/stoves and appliances.
- Make sure everyone is out of the building.
- Turn off the lights.
- Lock the doors.

CHAPTER 10

Elise's Tea Room Recipes

Salads

Elise's House Salad

Ingredients:

    Romaine lettuce
    Red cabbage
    Pecans
    Blue cheese

Mandarin oranges
Raspberry vinaigrette dressing

Preparation:

Chop lettuce and red cabbage and put into a large colander. Rinse and toss.
Place onto salad plates.
Garnish with pecans, blue cheese, and mandarin oranges as desired.
Drizzle with raspberry vinaigrette dressing.

Melinda's Chicken Salad

Ingredients:

    Grilled marinated chicken breast or curry chicken breast
    Romaine lettuce
    Red cabbage
    Pecans
    Blue cheese
    Mandarin oranges
    Raspberry vinaigrette dressing

Preparation:

Chop lettuce and red cabbage and put into a large colander. Rinse and toss.
Place onto salad plates.
Garnish with pecans, blue cheese, and mandarin oranges as desired.
Drizzle with raspberry vinaigrette dressing.
Place grilled or curry chicken breast on top of salad.

Tea Sandwiches

Chicken Curry Tea Sandwiches

Ingredients:

    4 chicken breasts
    2 tablespoons curry powder
    2 tablespoons sweet basil
    2 tablespoons garlic salt
    2 tablespoons poultry seasoning
    Salt and pepper to taste
    Mayonnaise to taste
    Wheat bread, 20 slices or one loaf of bread

Preparation:

Put the chicken in a large pot. Add water, garlic salt, poultry seasoning, and salt and pepper.
Bring to boil; reduce heat and simmer for 20 minutes until fully cooked.
Drain liquid and let chicken cool. Cut into small cubes.
In a large bowl, combine chicken, curry powder, sweet basil, and mayonnaise to taste.
Spread mayonnaise on two slices of wheat bread. Add chicken mixture between slices.
Cut off crust and cut into four triangles.
Makes 40 tea sandwiches.

Egg Salad Tea Sandwiches

Ingredients:

    12 large boiled eggs
    1 teaspoon salt
    1 teaspoon pepper
    Yellow mustard (e.g., Heinz)
    Mayonnaise
    White bread, 20 slices or one loaf of bread

Preparation:

    Chop eggs and place in a large bowl.
    Add salt and pepper, mustard, and mayonnaise (to taste); mix.
    Spread mayonnaise on two slices of white bread.
    Spread egg mixture between slices.
    Cut off crust and cut into four triangles.
    Makes 40 tea sandwiches.

Cucumber Tea Sandwiches

Ingredients:

    1 English or hothouse cucumber
    1 package soft cream cheese (or herb cream cheese)
    2 tablespoons white vinegar
    Dill
    White bread, 20 slices or one whole loaf

Preparation:

    Cut cucumber into 1/8-inch slices.
    Place cucumber into a bowl with white vinegar and dill.
    Spread soft cream cheese on two slices of white bread.
    Add cucumber between bread slices.
    Cut off crust and cut into four triangles.
    Makes 40 tea sandwiches.

Chive Tea Sandwiches

Ingredients:

    Fresh chives
    Soft cream cheese
    White bread, 20 slices or one whole loaf

Preparation:

    Chop chives into 1/4-inch pieces.
    Spread soft cream cheese on two slices of bread.
    Sprinkle a generous amount of chives onto the cream cheese.
    Cut off crust and cut into four triangles.
    Makes 40 tea sandwiches.

Apple Pecan Tea Sandwiches

Ingredients:

    1 can apple pie mix
    1/2 cup chopped pecans
    1 package soft cream cheese
    Apple raisin cinnamon bread, 8 slices or one loaf of bread

Preparation:

    Chop apple mix into small pieces and add in pecans.
    Spread soft cream cheese on two slices of apple cinnamon bread.
    Place apple and pecan mixture between slices.
    Cut off crust and cut in half.
    Makes 16 tea sandwiches.

Elise Benavidez

Black Olive Tea Sandwiches

Ingredients:

    2 cups black olive slices
    1/4 cup green olives stuffed with pimentos
    1 garlic clove
    1/4 cup olive oil
    1/4 cup Parmesan cheese
    1 package soft cream cheese
    Rye bread, 18 slices or one whole loaf

Preparation:

    In a food processor, blend black olives, green olives, garlic clove, olive oil, and Parmesan cheese.
    Spread olive mixture on one slice of rye bread; spread soft cream cheese on another. Put slices together.
    Cut off crust and cut into 3 slices.
    Makes 27 tea sandwiches.

Scones

Grandmother's Traditional Scones

Ingredients:

    4 cups all-purpose flour
    1 tablespoon salt
    2 tablespoons baking powder
    2 tablespoons vegetable oil
    4 cups cake flour
    1 teaspoon cream of tarter
    11/2 sticks of butter, softened
    2 cups milk
    4 eggs

Elise Benavidez

Preparation:

Preheat oven to 325°.
Mix flour, cake flour, cream of tartar, baking powder, and salt in bowl. Add oil and butter; mix.
Separate one egg white into a small bowl; add a few drops of water and mix for egg wash. Set aside.
Add the remaining yolk and other eggs to the flour and butter mixture; mix.
Add milk and mix batter until it's not too wet or dry, adding more milk or flour if needed.
Mix with a gentle motion. Over mixing will result in dense scones.
Roll out on a wooden board and cut with cutter.
Put scones on cookie sheet (one sheet holds 15 scones).
Gently and lightly brush the scones with the egg wash.
Bake at 325° in convection oven for 19 minutes or conventional oven for 30–35 minutes.
Serve hot.
Can be frozen if not used immediately.
Makes approximately 20 3-inch scones.

Elise's Tea Room and Recipes

Chocolate Chip Scones

Ingredients:

    4 cups premixed baking mix
    2 cups white cake flour
    2 cups pastry flour
    2 cups semisweet chocolate chips
    2/3 cup sugar
    12 tablespoons butter or 11/2 sticks, softened
    1/4 cup vanilla
    13/4 cup milk (may add more if needed)
    1 egg

Preparation:

Preheat oven to 325°.
Mix baking mix, cake flour, pastry flour, and sugar in bowl.
Add egg and mix.
Add softened butter and mix.
Add chocolate chips.
Add milk and vanilla and lightly mix until dough is no longer sticky.
Roll out on a flour-dusted wooden board and cut with cookie cutter.
Place on cookie sheet (one sheet holds 15 scones).
Bake at 325° for 19 minutes in convection oven or 30–35 minutes in conventional oven until golden brown.
Makes 24 scones.

Lemon Scones

4 cups premixed baking mix
2 cups pastry flour
2 cups lemon cake flour
Juice and zest of 1 lemon (Meyer lemon is best)
2 drops of yellow food coloring (if desired, for color)
2/3 cup sugar
12 tablespoons butter or 1 1/2 sticks, softened
1 2/3 cups milk
1 egg

Preparation:

> Preheat oven to 325°.
> Mix baking mix, pastry flour, cake flour, and sugar in bowl.
> Add butter to flour mixture; mix.
> Add egg and mix.
> Combine lemon juice, food coloring, and milk.
> Add mixture to flour and fold gently until no longer sticky (add flour if needed).
> Roll out on wooden board and cut with cookie cutter.
> Put scones on cookie sheet (one sheet holds 15 scones).
> Bake at 325° for 19 minutes in convection oven or 30–35 minutes in conventional oven until golden brown.
> Makes 24 scones.

Cranberry Scones

Ingredients:

4 cups premixed baking mix
2 cups pastry flour
2 cups cake flour
3/4 cup sugar
2 cups sweetened dried cranberries
12 tablespoons butter or 1 1/2 sticks, softened
1/4 cup vanilla
1 egg
1 3/4 cups milk

Elise Benavidez

Preparation:

>Preheat oven to 325°.
>Mix baking mix, pastry flour, cake flour, and sugar in bowl.
>Add butter to flour mixture; mix.
>Add egg and mix.
>Add cranberries and mix.
>Combine milk and vanilla.
>Add milk mixture to flour and fold gently until no longer sticky (add flour if needed)
>Roll out on wooden board and cut with cookie cutter.
>Put scones on cookie sheet (one sheet holds 15 scones).
>Bake at 325° for 19 minutes in convection oven or 30–35 minutes in conventional oven until golden brown.
>Makes 24 scones.

Elise's Tea Room and Recipes

Strawberry Scones

Ingredients:

    4 cups premixed baking mix
    2 cups pastry flour
    2 cups cake flour
    2/3 cup sugar
    16 tablespoons butter or 1 1/2 sticks, softened
    1 egg
    2 cups fresh strawberries, chopped
    1 3/4 cups milk
    1/4 cup Torani strawberry syrup

Preparation:

> Preheat oven to 325°.
> Mix baking mix, pastry flour, cake flour, and sugar in bowl.
> Add butter to flour mixture; mix.
> Add egg and mix.
> Add chopped strawberries and mix.
> Combine milk and strawberry syrup.
> Add milk mixture to flour and fold gently until no longer sticky (add flour if needed).
> Roll out on wooden board and cut with cookie cutter.
> Put scones on cookie sheet (one sheet holds 15 scones).
> Bake at 325° for 19 minutes in convection oven or 30–35 minutes in conventional oven until golden brown.
> Makes 24 scones.

Pumpkin Scones

Ingredients:

    4 cups premixed baking mix
    2 cups pastry flour
    2 cups cake flour
    2/3 cup sugar
    16 tablespoons butter or 1 1/2 sticks, softened
    1 egg
    2 tablespoons cinnamon
    1 teaspoon ground cloves
    1 can pumpkin pie mix
    Milk, if needed

Preparation:

> Preheat oven to 325°.
> Mix baking mix, pastry flour, cake flour, cinnamon, cloves, and sugar in bowl.
> Add butter to flour mixture; mix.
> Add egg and mix.
> Add pumpkin pie mix and fold gently until no longer sticky (add milk if needed).
> Roll out on wooden board and cut with cookie cutter.
> Put scones on cookie sheet (one sheet holds 15 scones).
> Bake at 325° for 19 minutes in convection oven or 30–35 minutes in conventional oven until golden brown.
> Makes 24 scones.

Elise's Devonshire Cream

Ingredients:

    1 pint heavy whipping cream
    6 tablespoons powdered sugar
    6 tablespoons cream cheese
    2 tablespoons lemon juice

Preparation:

Place all ingredients in mixing bowl.
Start mixer at low speed, increasing speed slowly until on high. Continue mixing on high until holes and gaps appear in the mixture.
Use immediately or transfer to airtight container and refrigerate.
Serves 20

Lemon Curd

Ingredients:

    1 cup freshly squeezed lemon juice
    Zest of 2 lemons
    2 sticks butter, softened
    5 egg yolks
    5 whole eggs
    1 3/4 cups sugar

Preparation:

Bring butter, sugar, lemon juice, and zest to a boil in a pot.
Whip eggs and egg yolks into a homogeneous mixture.
Slowly add approximately 1/4 of the hot butter and sugar mixture to the egg mixture and whisk briskly (to temper the eggs).
Remove the pot from the heat. Add the tempered eggs to the rest of the mixture in the pot. Return the pot to the burner and stir vigorously.
Remove the pot from the heat when the mixture becomes thick and lightly boils, about 3 minutes.
Chill before serving
Serves 65

Soups

Cream of Asparagus Soup

Ingredients:

    22 small asparagus stalks or one bunch
    1/2 onion, chopped
    8 cups chicken broth
    1 cup flour
    1 stick butter
    1 can evaporated milk

Preparation:

In a medium saucepan, melt 2/3 stick of butter.
Add flour and stir to make a roux.
Place chicken broth in a large pot; whisk in roux. Simmer.
In a medium saucepan, sauté chopped onion in 1/3 stick of butter until translucent.
Chop asparagus into small pieces.
Add asparagus and onion to chicken broth and bring to boil.
Simmer on low for 1 hour or until asparagus is cooked (stir often).
Add evaporated milk.
Keep warm until serving or freeze for later use.
Makes 20 1-cup servings.

Lobster Bisque

Ingredients:

    2 lobster tails
    1 cup flour
    1 stick butter
    1 garlic clove, finely chopped
    2 1-quart (14-ounce) cans seafood broth (may use clam juice)
    2 tablespoons Old Bay seasoning
    1 can evaporated milk
    Dill (garnish; optional)
    Parsley (garnish; optional)
    Sour cream (garnish; optional)

Preparation:

In a large pot, combine seafood broth and 4 cups of water; simmer.
In a medium saucepan, melt 2/3 stick of butter.
Add flour and mix to make a roux.
Whisk roux into broth.
Rinse lobster, cut down middle, and remove meat.
In a medium saucepan, sauté lobster shell, lobster meat, Old Bay seasoning, and garlic in 1/3 stick butter until shells are bright pink.
Add to broth and simmer for 1 hour.
Add evaporated milk.
Remove shells and puree soup in food processor.
Garnish with dill, parsley, and/or sour cream, if desired.
Makes 20 1-cup servings.

Quiches

Spinach Quiche

Ingredients:

    2 cups heavy cream
    2 cups milk
    1 tablespoon garlic salt
    9 large eggs
    2 cups (8 ounces) shredded cheddar jack cheese
    One bunch of fresh baby spinach
    1 clove garlic, finely chopped
    1 tablespoons butter
    2 8-inch pie shells, prebaked

Preparation:

Preheat oven to 300° for convection oven or 325° for conventional oven.
Sauté spinach in butter and garlic until wilted.
In a large bowl, whisk eggs; add garlic salt. Whisk in milk and heavy cream.
Add 1 cup cheese to each shell.
Add half of the cooked spinach to each shell.
Add half of the egg, milk, and heavy cream mixture to each shell.
Bake for 30 minutes in convection oven or 45 minutes in conventional oven until golden brown.
Note: You can use this procedure to make Ortega and bacon quiches.
Makes 12 servings.

Elise's Tea Room and Recipes

Desserts

Grandmother's Peach Cobbler

Elise Benavidez

Grandmother's Peach Cobbler

Ingredients:

   1 stick butter
   1 cup sugar
   1 cup flour
   3/4 cup milk
   2 teaspoons baking powder
   Salt, pinch
   4 cups of fresh peaches sprinkled with 2 tablespoons of sugar (or l large can of peaches, not drained)
   Brown sugar and cinnamon (optional)

Preparation:

   Preheat oven to 350°.
   Melt butter in a baking dish or casserole dish.
   In a bowl, combine sugar, flour, milk, baking powder, and salt into a batter.
   Pour batter into the baking dish with melted butter.
   Place the fruit evenly on top of the batter.
   As it cooks, the crust rises to the top.
   Bake for 1 hour at 350°.
   Sprinkle brown sugar and cinnamon on top, if desired.
   Makes 6 servings.

Elise's Tea Room and Recipes

Grandmother's Shortbread Cookies

Ingredients:

    2 sticks unsalted butter, softened
    1/2 cup powdered sugar
    1 teaspoon pure vanilla extract
    2 cups all-purpose flour

Preparation:

    Preheat oven to 350°.
    Mix flour and salt with whisk and set aside.
    With a mixer, cream the butter, about 1 minute.
    Add the sugar; beat until smooth. Stir in vanilla.
    Gently stir in the flour mixture until blended.
    Roll out dough into a circle and wrap in plastic wrap.

Refrigerate for 1 hour.
Lightly flour cutting board; roll out dough to 1/4-inch thick.
Cut dough using cookie cutters. Place cookies on baking sheet and chill for 15 minutes.
Bake at 350° for 8–10 minutes or until cookies are light brown.
Cookies can be frozen after baking.
Makes approximately 20 shortbread cookies.

Using a cookie cutter, you can make shortbread cookies in different shapes for the holidays.

Elise's Tea Room and Recipes

In honor of my father-in-law, I would like to included one of his recipes.

Jesse M. Benavidez, 1923–2010

Father-in-Law's Enchiladas

Ingredients:

    12 corn tortillas
    1/4 cup vegetable oil
    1 28-ounce can mild or hot enchilada sauce

1 8-ounce can tomato sauce
1 tablespoons cornstarch
4 cups Mexican cheese or(shredded cheddar jack)
1 small can sliced black olives
1 onion, chopped (optional)

Preparation:

Preheat oven to 425°.
In a saucepan, combine enchilada sauce, tomato sauce, and cornstarch. Bring to a low simmer.
In a frying pan, sauté onion in 2 tablespoons of oil until translucent.
In a frying pan, heat vegetable oil and fry each tortilla until soft; drain on paper towel.
Pour a small amount of the sauce into a greased 9x13 casserole dish.
One at a time, dip each tortilla into the pot of sauce, covering both sides.
Place sauce-covered tortillas in the casserole dish and add cheese, onions, black olives, and 1 tablespoon of sauce; roll up.
Repeat for the rest of the tortillas.
Pour remaining sauce over tortillas. Sprinkle with remaining cheese and black olives.
Bake at 425° for 45 minutes until cheese is melted and bubbling.
Makes 12 enchiladas (serves 6).

Elise's Tea Room and Recipes

ELISE BENAVIDEZ OPENED Elise's Tea Room in 1996, and she is the executive chef and owner. This female-run business is located in the Bixby Knolls neighborhood of Long Beach, California. The Southern California Restaurant Writers have awarded the tea room with their Gold Award for the last ten years. In Washington, DC, Benavidez was recognized as Businesswoman of the Year and appointed to the Small Business Commission. Elise's Tea Room was recently given the Certificate of Recognition by the U.S. Congress for the participation and Sponsorship of the city's cultural events.

Elise has been married for thirty- two years to her sweetheart whom she captivated when she was eight years of age. She is proud of her and husband's Bixby Knolls Swing Dance Champions over forty-five, and newly acquired skateboard skills. Their boys and daughter-in- law have attained career accolades but not before all three worked at the tea room. Elise and husband Marcos have a long

Elise Benavidez

family history residence in Long Beach were fifteen to twenty times a year this close, huge and eclectic family gathers for events leading to the end of the year caroling. The family continues to grow and has been blessed with a granddaughter, the light of their life.

Made in the USA
Columbia, SC
24 April 2017